THE
5 LOVE LANGUAGES®

WORKBOOK

THE 5 LOVE LANGUAGES®

#1 *NEW YORK TIMES* BESTSELLER

Gary Chapman

WORKBOOK

NORTHFIELD PUBLISHING

CHICAGO

© 2023 by
Gary Chapman

Developed with the assistance of Peachtree Publishing Services (www.peachtreeeditorial.com). Special thanks to Randy Southern.
Interior design: Erik M. Peterson
Cover design: Faceout Studio
Cover image of bokeh copyright © 2023 by Ole moda/Shutterstock (1469341238). All rights reserved.

ISBN: 978-0-8024-3296-4

We hope you enjoy this book from Northfield Publishing. Our goal is to provide high-quality, thought-provoking books and products that connect truth to your real needs and challenges. For more information on other books and products that will help you with all your important relationships, go to northfieldpublishing.com or write to:

Northfield Publishing
820 N. LaSalle Boulevard
Chicago, IL 60610

1 3 5 7 9 10 8 6 4 2

Printed in the United States of America

CONTENTS

INTRODUCTION

WELCOME to a labor of love.

The twelve lessons in this book were created for one purpose: to strengthen and deepen your loving relationship with your husband or wife. The process won't be easy. Nothing worthwhile ever is. This study will pose some challenging questions. It will take you outside your comfort zone. It will even require you to do homework.

But this isn't busywork. These lessons give you workable strategies for applying the principles of *The 5 Love Languages*. They offer glimpses of your relationship's potential when you and your spouse speak each other's love languages.

If you're working through this study alone, take heart. Your solo efforts will likely have a profound impact on your relationship. Throughout *The 5 Love Languages*, you'll find accounts of extremely dysfunctional relationships that not only survived but thrived thanks to one partner's commitment to learning his or her spouse's love language.

If you're working through this study as a couple, let patience, grace, and humor be your companions. Learning a new love language can be difficult, and there's more than a little trial and error involved. Show your appreciation for your spouse's efforts to communicate love in ways that are meaningful to you, no matter how clumsy those efforts are at first. And be sure to let him or her know when those efforts hit the mark.

If you're working through this study in a group, pay attention to what your fellow group members share. Inspiration and wisdom can be found in unexpected places. In your interactions with group members, be generous with your encouragement and sparing with your criticism. Ask appropriate follow-up questions to show your interest in other couples' success. See *The 5 Love Languages* Leader's Guide on pages 106–107 for helpful suggestions in facilitating group discussions.

Regardless of how you approach this study, you should be aware that the lessons in this book will require a significant investment of time and effort. There's a lot of important material in these pages. But it's virtually a risk-free investment. You will see dividends. And the more of yourself you pour into this workbook, the greater your dividends will be.

Enjoy the journey!

GARY CHAPMAN

OBJECTIVE

In reading this chapter, you will learn how becoming fluent in your spouse's primary love language helps you "work smarter" in showing love in a meaningful way.

WHAT HAPPENS TO LOVE AFTER THE WEDDING?

INSTRUCTIONS: Complete this first lesson after reading chapter 1 ("What Happens to Love After the Wedding?" pp. 11–16) of *The 5 Love Languages*.

KEY TERMS

Love languages: five distinct methods people use to communicate and receive emotional love.

Primary love language: the love language that most profoundly impacts a person and causes him or her to feel loved.

OPENING QUESTIONS

1. What's been your experience in learning—or trying to learn—a second language? How adept were you in learning the language? What were your biggest challenges?

2. Understanding love languages involves celebrating our differences. In what ways are you and your spouse different? Which differences present the biggest challenge?

THINK ABOUT IT

3. In chapter 1, Dr. Chapman tells the story of a man he met on an airplane. What red flags do you see in the man's relationship history that highlight the need to learn our spouse's primary love language?

4. Put yourself in the man's position. You find yourself seated next to a renowned relationship expert who invites you to share your relationship history with him. What would you tell him? How would you summarize your major romantic relationships? What common threads do you think Dr. Chapman would find in those relationships?

5. **"Keeping love alive in our marriages is serious business."** That's why, as Dr. Chapman explains, you can find advice in countless books, articles, TV and radio shows, and websites. List some of the pros and cons of turning to these sources for relationship advice.

6. Dr. Chapman writes, **"Most of us grow up learning the language of our parents and siblings, which becomes our *primary* or native tongue."** That goes not just for verbal and written language but, to a certain extent, for love languages as well. Who were the primary influences on your love language? Who shaped your thinking about what it means to show love to someone else? In what areas do you see their influence on your life?

7. No one would expect you to become fluent in Portuguese in a week, a month, or even a year. The same goes for becoming fluent in a second love language. Why is trial and error an important part of becoming fluent in your spouse's primary love language?

8. **"Seldom do a husband and wife have the same primary emotional love language. We tend to speak our primary love language, and we become confused when our spouse does not understand what we are communicating."** This reality check from Dr. Chapman highlights the challenge couples face when it comes to giving and receiving love in meaningful ways. On a scale of one to ten, with one being "Mass Confusion" and ten being "Perfect Understanding," how would you rate you and your spouse's emotional communication? How do you think your husband or wife would rate it? Where do you see room for improvement?

9. According to Dr. Chapman, what is the key to a long-lasting, loving marriage? What steps can you take to prepare for the challenge involved?

TAKE IT HOME

Thomas Edison once said, "I have not failed. I've just found 10,000 ways that won't work." In your relationship with your spouse, you've probably found several different ways of showing love that didn't work as you'd hoped. That doesn't mean you failed—not if you learned something from them.

In the table below, list a few strategies you've used to show love to your husband or wife. Write down how they responded to each one, how you reacted to their response, and what you took away from each experience.

For example, maybe you once planned a romantic evening, complete with candlelight, soft music, petals—the works. Instead of being wowed, however, maybe your spouse just played along to spare your feelings. That may have left you feeling annoyed or embarrassed. Your takeaway may have been that what works in romantic movies doesn't always work in real life.

STRATEGY	YOUR SPOUSE'S RESPONSE	YOUR REACTION	YOUR TAKEAWAY

THE TREK BEGINS

You're about to embark on a life-changing journey with your spouse. Before you do, take a few minutes to assess where you are right now. Give yourself a baseline you can use months and years from now to measure the growth of your relationship.

Describe your relationship with your husband or wife as it stands right now.

What's your motivation for beginning this study?

What's your ideal outcome? What do you want to happen as a result of this study?

What strengths do you possess that will help you achieve your goal?

What challenges do you foresee in applying the principles of *The 5 Love Languages* in your relationship?

LOVE CHALLENGE

Communication is the key to success in learning to show love to your spouse in a meaningful way. What specific questions will you ask your husband or wife this week to help guide your efforts to learn their primary love language?

Use this space for more notes, quotes, or lessons learned from the chapter.

OBJECTIVE

In reading this chapter, you will learn how the emptiness or fullness
of our "love tank" affects our emotional well-being.

KEEPING THE LOVE TANK FULL

INSTRUCTIONS: Complete this second lesson after reading chapter 2 ("Keeping the Love Tank Full," pp. 19–24) of *The 5 Love Languages*.

KEY TERM

Love tank: the emotional reservoir inside everyone that is filled when people speak to us in our primary love language.

OPENING QUESTIONS

1. If you wanted to really make an impression on your spouse, to do something he or she would remember fondly for a long time, what would you do? Why would that be special to them?

2. What if your effort to do something special didn't have the desired result? What if your husband or wife was underwhelmed by your attempt? How would you react?

THINK ABOUT IT

3. Dr. Chapman says, **"For love, we will climb mountains, cross seas, traverse desert sands, and endure untold hardships. Without love, mountains become unclimbable, seas uncrossable, deserts unbearable, and hardships our lot in life."** What have you done *for love*? Think of the big things and the small, the extreme and the mundane. How did they work out? Would you do them again? If so, which ones, and why?

4. **"Child psychologists affirm that every child has certain basic emotional needs that must be met if he is to be emotionally stable. Among those emotional needs, none is more basic than the need for love and affection, the need to sense that he or she belongs and is wanted."** With these words of Dr. Chapman in mind, how can you tell whether your need for love and affection is being met? What does emotional stability—the feeling that you belong and are wanted—look like in your life?

5. Dr. Ross Campbell introduced the metaphor of an "emotional tank" inside every person. The need to have that tank filled with love begins in childhood and has a very real impact on our behavior. What happens to children who receive an adequate supply of affection versus those who don't?

6. How do those childhood needs follow us into adulthood and marriage? According to Dr. Chapman, what is at the heart of marital desires? How does that coincide with the ancient biblical writings of a husband and wife becoming "one flesh"?

7. A husband expressed his frustration with his empty emotional tank by asking, "What good is the house, the cars, the place at the beach, or any of the rest of it if your wife doesn't love you?" A wife expressed hers by saying, "He ignores me all day long and then wants to jump in bed with me. I hate it." How might you or your spouse have expressed your frustration during a low point in your relationship?

8. Dr. Chapman writes, **"I am convinced that keeping the emotional love tank full is as important to a marriage as maintaining the proper oil level is to an automobile. Running your marriage on an empty 'love tank' may cost you even more than trying to drive your car without oil."** Oil reduces friction; it keeps the many different parts of a car running smoothly. How does the right kind of loving action do the same for a marriage?

9. Dr. Chapman "warns" of radically changed behavior when people's love tanks are full. Dreaming big, what radical changes would you like to see in your relationship with your husband or wife as you learn how to keep each other's love tanks filled?

TAKE IT HOME

Everyone's emotional needs are different. What fills your love tank may not fill your spouse's. Draw an arrow on each of the following fuel gauges to indicate how much that specific loving gesture would fill your emotional love tank.

You overhear your spouse telling someone how amazingly creative you are.

Your spouse postpones his or her own plans in order to spend the day with you before you leave for a weeklong trip.

Your spouse gives you a framed photo of the two of you on your first date.

Your spouse spends an entire Saturday afternoon cleaning your car, inside and out.

Your spouse gives you an impromptu back rub.

A BIG DIFFERENCE

A person whose love tank is full experiences life in a much different way from someone whose love tank is empty. The fullness or emptiness of your tank affects the way you approach and enjoy even the most common daily activities, including the five listed below. Imagine how each activity might play out when your love tank is full versus when your love tank is empty.

For example, if you're out to dinner with your husband or wife with a full love tank, you might talk excitedly about what happened at work or what's going on in your family. You might laugh a lot, hold hands across the table, and flirt shamelessly with each other. With an empty love tank, you might spend most of your time checking your phones and struggling to make small talk.

ACTIVITY	WITH A FULL LOVE TANK	WITH AN EMPTY LOVE TANK
Going out to dinner with your spouse		
Coming home from work		
Spending time with friends		
Planning your weekend		
Getting ready for bed		

LOVE CHALLENGE

Learning how to fill your husband's or wife's love tank will require you to have some potentially difficult, but ultimately helpful, conversations. What questions will you ask them this week to help initiate those conversations?

Use this space for more notes, quotes, or lessons learned from the chapter.

OBJECTIVE

In reading this chapter, you will learn how to appreciate the excitement
of falling in love while still recognizing the importance of moving past
the in-love stage to embrace real love.

FALLING IN LOVE

INSTRUCTIONS: Complete this third lesson after reading chapter 3 ("Falling in Love," pp. 27–35) of *The 5 Love Languages*.

KEY TERM

In-love experience: a euphoric emotional obsession in which a person fixates on the positive aspects of a romantic partner—and of the relationship—but loses sight of practical realities.

OPENING QUESTIONS

1. What do you remember about being "in love" for the first time?

2. When did you know the "in-love" experience had become the real thing when you were dating your spouse? At what point did you both know it was reciprocal and begin to talk about marriage?

THINK ABOUT IT

3. The late psychologist Dr. Dorothy Tennov conducted long-range studies on the "in-love" experience. What did she conclude is the average life span of a romantic obsession? What factor might make it last a little longer? What happens at the end of that life span?

4. **"Welcome to the real world of marriage"** is how Dr. Chapman announces the stage that follows falling in love. According to him, what does the real world of marriage involve? What does the real world of marriage look like in your relationship?

5. Dr. Chapman writes, **"Some couples believe that the end of the 'in-love' experience means they have only two options."** What are those two options? What did the generation that chose the second option discover, as opposed to the previous generation, which chose the former option?

6. What does Dr. Chapman identify as a third and better alternative? How does "real love" differ from the "in-love experience"?

7. Dr. Chapman points out that real love **"requires effort and discipline."** For someone who is falling in love, the idea of having to put effort and discipline into a relationship may seem unromantic. On the contrary, why does that effort and discipline demonstrate something stronger, longer lasting, and more meaningful than the in-love stage?

8. According to Dr. Chapman, **"the emotional need for love must be met if we are to have emotional health."** What are some of the specific emotional needs that must be met? Most of those needs are met during the in-love stage. What mistake do many couples make during that time?

9. How can speaking your spouse's emotional love language change the emotional climate of your marriage? How can it help you recapture some of the magic of your original in-love experience?

TAKE IT HOME

Dr. Chapman emphasizes that what we see when we fall in love isn't always reality. The in-love experience can cause us to overlook some less-than-ideal aspects of our partner. Here's an exercise to draw attention to this phenomenon.

On the first outline, write down the things you notice in another person when you're falling in love. For example, you might draw an arrow to the side of the head and write, "Ears that listen intently when I talk about my day at work." Or you might draw an arrow to the chest and write, "A heart for rescue animals."

On the second outline, write down the things you don't notice in another person when you're falling in love. For example, you might draw an arrow to the mouth and write, "Words that seem overly harsh and controlling sometimes." Or you might draw arrows to the hands and write, "Hands that haven't worked a day in the past six months."

PEAKS AND VALLEYS

Use a graph to chart the highs and lows of your relationship with your husband or wife. Start with the year you met each other and continue to present day. Mark the highs, including your "in-love" experience, and your lows. Write down a word or phrase to explain each shift in your relationship. For example, a drop from the peaks of the early days of your relationship to a decade-long plateau might be explained by the challenges of parenting young children. A further drop to a valley might be explained by a sudden loss, a serious illness, joblessness, or some other crisis.

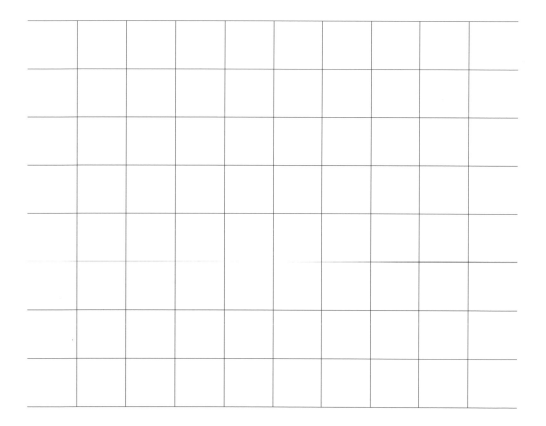

LOVE CHALLENGE

Sometimes two people fall in love because they start out speaking each other's primary love language, perhaps without even realizing it. But as the relationship changes, so do the emotional languages the couple speaks. And they lose something—again, perhaps without even realizing it. So when you want to learn each other's primary love language in earnest, it may be helpful to think back to the beginning of your relationship, to the in-love stage. What questions will you ask your husband or wife this week to help recall specifics of the in-love stage of your relationship?

Use this space for more notes, quotes, or lessons learned from the chapter.

OBJECTIVE

reading this chapter, you will learn how to use words of affirmation to express love in ways that fill your spouse's love tank.

LOVE LANGUAGE #1: WORDS OF AFFIRMATION

INSTRUCTIONS: Complete this fourth lesson after reading chapter 4 ("Love Language #1: Words of Affirmation," pp. 37–53) of *The 5 Love Languages*.

KEY TERM

Words of affirmation: verbal and written expressions of love, appreciation, and encouragement that communicate love in profound ways for people who speak that love language.

OPENING QUESTIONS

1. What is the best thing anyone has ever said to you? Who said it? What were the circumstances? What did those words mean to you when you first heard them? What, if any, lasting impact have they had on your life?

2. What is the most heartfelt compliment you've ever given someone else? What prompted you to say it? How did the person react? How did their reaction make you feel?

THINK ABOUT IT

3. According to Dr. Chapman, **"all of us have areas in which we feel insecure. We lack courage, and that lack of courage often hinders us from accomplishing the positive things that we would like to do. The latent potential within your spouse in his or her areas of insecurity may await your encouraging words."** What latent potential do you see in your spouse? What might your spouse accomplish if he or she could get past his or her insecurity? Give some examples of encouraging words that might help your husband or wife unlock their potential.

4. In Dr. Chapman's story about Keith and Allison, what were the words of affirmation that unlocked Allison's potential? Why were they so meaningful in that situation? What immediate and long-range impact did they have? How does it make you feel to know that your words can have a similar impact on your spouse?

5. Dr. Chapman writes, **"The manner in which we speak is exceedingly important. An ancient sage once said, 'A soft answer turns away anger.'"** How can kind words defuse potentially explosive situations with your husband or wife? Give some examples of how kindness can be expressed as much in what we don't say as in what we do say.

6. **"Love makes requests, not demands."** These words of Dr. Chapman emphasize the importance of humility in speaking words of affirmation. What might humble words sound like in your relationship?

7. Dr. Chapman is emphatic in saying, **"I am not suggesting verbal flattery in order to get your spouse to do something you want. The object of love is not getting something you want but doing something for the well-being of the one you love."** Why is it important for your words of affirmation to be separate from the requests you make of your spouse? How can you make sure that your words of affirmation aren't mistaken for manipulative flattery?

8. Mark Twain said, "I can live for two months on a good compliment." But what if the goal wasn't merely to live but to thrive? How many heartfelt compliments per month, per week, or per day would it take for someone whose primary love language is words of affirmation to live his or her best possible life?

9. To paraphrase the question Dr. Chapman poses at the beginning of the chapter: What would happen to the emotional climate of your marriage if you and your husband or wife heard words of affirmation regularly?

TAKE IT HOME

Gathering the material you need to speak words of affirmation is as easy as noticing and appreciating your spouse's many praiseworthy qualities. On the fruit tree below, identify various characteristics, gifts, and skills that your husband or wife possesses. These are areas that are ripe for words of affirmation. You can start with the low-hanging fruit—the easy ones. These are characteristics that are obvious to most people—beauty, sense of style, kindness, sense of humor. The upper branches of the tree are qualities that other people might not see—tenderness, vulnerability, a penchant for doing good things without anyone else noticing.

TO BE MORE SPECIFIC

Any genuine word of affirmation has the potential to fill someone's love tank, at a least a little. But the more specific and on-target our words are, the bigger their impact will be. In the chart below, you'll find some generic words of affirmation. Come up with a more specific way of expressing each one—a way that applies directly to your spouse. Your goal is to come up with a sentence or two that will have maximum impact on your partner.

You are attractive.

You work hard.

You have a kind heart.

You have a good sense of humor.

You make me happy.

You are a good spouse.

You are a good parent.

You are a good friend.

LOVE CHALLENGE

The key to effectively speaking the love language of words of affirmation is to be prepared to say the right thing to your husband or wife, in the right way, at the right time. What specific steps can you take this week to prepare and use words of affirmation?

STEP 1

STEP 2

STEP 3

STEP 4

STEP 5

STEP 6

Use this space for more notes, quotes, or lessons learned from the chapter.

OBJECTIVE

In reading this chapter, you will learn how to use quality time and quality conversation to express love in ways that fill your spouse's love tank.

LOVE LANGUAGE #2: QUALITY TIME

INSTRUCTIONS: Complete this fifth lesson after reading chapter 5 ("Love Language #2: Quality Time," pp. 55–72) of *The 5 Love Languages*.

KEY TERMS

Quality time: a way of expressing love through spending purposeful time with, and directing your full attention to, another person.

Quality conversation: empathetic dialogue in which two people share their experiences, thoughts, feelings, and desires in a friendly, uninterrupted context.

OPENING QUESTIONS

1. What principles and priorities guide your time management? How do you decide if something is worth your time?

2. What are some less-than-worthwhile things that compete for your time and keep you from doing the things you've prioritized?

THINK ABOUT IT

3. In the story Dr. Chapman tells at the beginning of the chapter, Mark makes a list of the things his wife, Andrea, would like the two of them to do together. This list is Mark's starting point in spending more quality time with Andrea. If you were to make a similar list, what would it include? What are some things your husband or wife would like the two of you to do together?

4. Dr. Chapman says, **"Quality time does not mean that we have to spend our together moments gazing into each other's eyes. It means that we are doing something together and that we are giving our full attention to the other person. The activity in which we are both engaged is incidental."** What steps can you take to help you give your full attention to your spouse for a concentrated period of time?

5. Dr. Chapman emphasizes that **"quality conversation is quite different from the first love language."** What is the key difference between quality conversation and words of affirmation? Which comes more naturally to you: words of affirmation, quality conversation, both, or neither? Explain.

6. Patrick's story of offering advice to his wife when she shared her problems at work reveals an important lesson for spouses trying to learn the dialect of quality conversation. What are some ways well-meaning spouses squander quality conversation opportunities without meaning to—or without even realizing it? Why does this present a special challenge for husbands or wives who see themselves as problem-solvers?

7. According to Dr. Chapman, what are some effective strategies for learning to listen in a meaningful way? What other suggestions would you add to the list? Dr. Chapman also compares learning to listen to learning a foreign language. In what ways are the two challenges similar? What would it take for you to become a fluent listener?

8. Dr. Chapman points out that learning to talk is as important to quality conversation as learning to listen. He identifies two different personality types—the Dead Sea and the Babbling Brook—to help us understand people's natural inclinations when it comes to talking. What's the difference between a Dead Sea personality and a Babbling Brook personality? What is the interaction like between the two personalities? How does establishing a daily sharing time promote quality conversation?

9. One of the dialects of the quality time love language is quality activities. According to Dr. Chapman, what are the three essential ingredients in a quality activity? How do you find time for quality activities in a busy schedule?

TAKE IT HOME

Below are three pie charts—one for a typical weekday, one for a typical Saturday, and one for a typical Sunday. Fill in each one to show (generally speaking) how you spend those twenty-four hours. The biggest pie pieces will likely be sleeping and work. Other categories might include school, household chores, exercise/training, screen time (TV, computer, and phone), family responsibilities, social engagements, and quality time with your spouse. Try to be as accurate as possible so that you get a good sense of where your time goes.

Typical Weekday   **Typical Saturday**   **Typical Sunday**

Below are three more pie charts. Fill them out again, this time with an eye toward carving out bigger pieces for quality time with your husband or wife. In what areas can you cut back so that you have more time to devote to filling your spouse's love tank?

Potential Weekday   **Potential Saturday**   **Potential Sunday**

UNI-TASKING

You'll probably encounter some challenges and obstacles as you learn to speak the love language of quality time. Keep in mind that none of those challenges or obstacles are insurmountable. To help you discover that for yourself, here are a few examples drawn from actual experiences. For each one, come up with a workable solution or strategy.

CHALLENGE	SOLUTION
I'm easily distracted.	
It's hard to find time in our schedules when we can be alone.	
Finding privacy in our home is nearly impossible, and leaving the house isn't always an option.	
I'm not a natural conversationalist, so I don't know what questions to ask.	
I feel like I'm sending the wrong signals if I pretend to be interested in something my spouse is saying when I'm really not.	
I'm uncomfortable with sharing my thoughts and emotions.	

LOVE CHALLENGE

Dr. Chapman says, **"One of the by-products of quality activities is that they provide a memory bank from which to draw in the years ahead."** What is one thing you can do with your spouse this week to create a happy memory?

Use this space for more notes, quotes, or lessons learned from the chapter.

In reading this chapter, you will learn how to use well-chosen gifts to express love in ways that fill your spouse's love tank.

LOVE LANGUAGE #3: RECEIVING GIFTS

INSTRUCTIONS: Complete this sixth lesson after reading chapter 6 ("Love Language #3: Receiving Gifts," pp. 75–89) of *The 5 Love Languages*.

KEY TERM

Receiving gifts: a love language in which a person experiences emotional wholeness through well-chosen presents.

OPENING QUESTIONS

1. What's the best gift you've ever received? Who gave it to you? What were the circumstances? What made the gift so special?

2. What are some underrated gifts that can be just as meaningful as big, expensive presents?

THINK ABOUT IT

3. In his anthropology fieldwork, Dr. Chapman discovered in every culture he studied that gift giving was part of the love-marriage process. What important questions does that discovery raise?

4. On the island of Dominica, Dr. Chapman met a man named Fred whose gift giving made a profound impact. What did Fred's two gifts have in common? What can we take away from the fact that Dr. Chapman still remembered them vividly decades later?

5. According to Dr. Chapman, the best way to begin to learn the love language of gift giving is to **"make a list of all the gifts your spouse has expressed excitement about receiving through the years. They may be gifts you have given or gifts given by other family members or friends. The list will give you an idea of the kind of gifts your spouse would enjoy receiving."** What gifts would be on your spouse's list?

6. Dr. Chapman writes, **"If you are to become an effective gift giver, you may have to change your attitude about money."** How do "spenders" and "savers" differ in their attitude toward gift giving? Why does it make sense to approach gift giving as an investment?

7. Dr. Chapman says, **"There is an intangible gift that sometimes speaks more loudly than a gift that can be held in one's hand."** What is that intangible gift? How does it become a symbol of your love?

8. Doug, the husband Dr. Chapman met after a marriage seminar in Chicago, committed to a weeklong effort of gift giving to connect with his wife, Kate. What gifts did he choose? How did Kate react to his gift giving? Why were his gifts especially meaningful to her—and to their children?

9. If you were to commit to a similar weeklong gift-giving effort for your spouse, what gifts would you choose? Why do you think those gifts would be especially meaningful? How do you think they would react? What difference might your weeklong effort make in your relationship?

TAKE IT HOME

In the spaces below, draw a few important gifts that you've either given or received and explain why each one is especially meaningful for you. For example, you might draw a souvenir your parent brought back from an international business trip. The gift may remind you that even though you were thousands of miles apart, you were never far from your parent's thoughts. Or you might draw a dandelion that your child gave you. The "flower" may be a heartwarming reminder of your child's innocent love of beauty and desire to share it with you.

A GIFT FOR EVERY OCCASION

If your spouse's primary love language is receiving gifts, you don't have to wait for special occasions—birthdays, Christmas, anniversaries—to express your love. Any time is a good time to give a thoughtful gift. The more appropriate the gift, the bigger its impact will be.

Here are a few nontraditional occasions in which the right gift could fill your husband's or wife's love tank. See if you can come up with an appropriate gift for each one. Keep in mind that you don't have to spend a lot of money to communicate love through gift giving. Sometimes you don't have to buy anything at all. Often, a simple, handmade gift can speak volumes.

Your spouse is having a bad week.

Your spouse reached an exercise goal.

Your spouse has been feeling nostalgic lately.

You and your spouse are starting a road trip.

Your spouse is preparing a major presentation.

It's Tuesday.

LOVE CHALLENGE

Dr. Chapman says, **"If you discover that your spouse's primary love language is receiving gifts, then perhaps you will understand that purchasing gifts for him or her is the best investment you can make."** What investment will you make in your spouse this week?

Use this space for more notes, quotes, or lessons learned from the chapter.

OBJECTIVE

In reading this chapter, you will learn how to perform tasks
and complete projects in ways that fill your spouse's love tank.

LOVE LANGUAGE #4: ACTS OF SERVICE

INSTRUCTIONS: Complete this seventh lesson after reading chapter 7 ("Love Language #4: Acts of Service," pp. 91–104) of *The 5 Love Languages.*

KEY TERM

Acts of service: a love language in which a person experiences emotional wholeness when chores or tasks are done for his or her benefit.

OPENING QUESTIONS

1. When you were young, what chores were you expected to do? What was your reward for doing them or your consequences for not doing them?

2. How do you and your spouse divvy up chores and household responsibilities in your home?

THINK ABOUT IT

3. Dr. Chapman's conversation with Dave and Mary reveals an important truth about relationships—namely, that the real source of conflict isn't always what it appears to be. What was Mary's major complaint about Dave? What was Dave's major complaint about Mary? What did Dr. Chapman see as the actual source of their conflict?

4. Dave and Mary's case is far from unusual. Most couples have a few core issues that rear their heads time and again in arguments. What are those core issues in your relationship? What topics come up again and again when you argue? Based on Dr. Chapman's conversation with Dave and Mary, what do you think he would conclude about your core issues of conflict?

5. Early in their relationship, Dave and Mary were filling each other's love tanks without even realizing it. Why did they gradually stop? Do you see any parallels in your own relationship? Were there things your spouse used to do that made you feel loved that he or she no longer does? Would they say there are things you used to do to fill their love tank that you no longer do? If so, why did you stop? What effect has it had on your relationship?

6. Dr. Chapman emphasizes, **"Love is a choice and cannot be coerced."** Criticizing and making demands of each other leaves little room for genuine expressions of love through acts of service. What is a more effective way for husbands and wives to make their needs known? What would that look like in your relationship?

7. Dr. Chapman says, **"Learning the love language of acts of service will require some of us to reexamine our stereotypes of the roles of husbands and wives."** Why do some stereotypes have an especially strong hold on our idea of what it means to be a husband or wife? What's the best strategy for breaking these stereotypes?

8. If Dr. Chapman asked you to make a list of three or four acts of service your husband or wife could do to make you feel loved, as he did with Dave and Mary, what would your list include? What would your spouse's list include?

9. Dr. Chapman summarizes the love language of acts of service this way: **"If your spouse's love language is acts of service, then 'actions speak louder than words.'"** What are the biggest obstacles you face in learning to communicate love through your actions? What is the best strategy for overcoming each one?

TAKE IT HOME

For better or worse, daily life in a household presents countless opportunities for acts of service. Rate the following chores according to how much you and your spouse dislike doing them (0 = Don't mind at all; 10 = Absolutely despise). Place an "X" on the line to indicate your feelings about that chore and an "O" to indicate their feelings.

Washing the dishes

0	1	2	3	4	5	6	7	8	9	10

Vacuuming the floor

0	1	2	3	4	5	6	7	8	9	10

Doing the laundry

0	1	2	3	4	5	6	7	8	9	10

Walking and picking up after pets

0	1	2	3	4	5	6	7	8	9	10

Doing yard work

0	1	2	3	4	5	6	7	8	9	10

Washing the car(s)

0	1	2	3	4	5	6	7	8	9	10

SEVEN TO START WITH

Make a list of seven specific chores that you can do for your husband or wife as acts of service. Assign a point value (1 to 10) to each chore, based on how much your spouse dislikes it and how much effort it will take on your part. For example, taking the dog for a quick walk on a beautiful spring day would probably be a "1" or "2," since there's not much to dislike about it and likely doesn't require much effort. On the other hand, taking the dog for a walk in the dead of winter might be an "8" or "9."

Once your list is complete, you have a starting point for doing acts of service. With the point values, you also have an idea of how big of an impact each act of service is likely to have. The higher the score, the fuller their love tank will be.

ACT OF SERVICE	POINT VALUE
1.	
2.	
3.	
4.	
5.	
6.	
7.	

LOVE CHALLENGE

Dr. Chapman writes, **"People tend to criticize their spouse most loudly in the area where they themselves have the deepest emotional need."** With that in mind, what seems to be your spouse's deepest emotional need right now? What specific act of service will you do this week to meet that need?

Use this space for more notes, quotes, or lessons learned from the chapter.

OBJECTIVE

In reading this chapter, you will learn how to use
physical touch in ways that fill your spouse's love tank.

LOVE LANGUAGE #5: PHYSICAL TOUCH

INSTRUCTIONS: Complete this eighth lesson after reading chapter 8 ("Love Language #5: Physical Touch," pp. 107–117) of *The 5 Love Languages.*

KEY TERM

Physical touch: a love language in which a person experiences emotional wholeness through human contact.

OPENING QUESTIONS

1. What are the most memorable physical touches you've ever experienced? Maybe it was your first kiss. Or holding the hand of a grandparent in a hospital bed. Or a bear hug from your mom the first time you came home from college. Or your spouse feeling your forehead to check for a fever when you were sick. List as many memorable touches as you can recall.

2. If someone offered you $50 to go an entire day without touching anyone, would you do it? What about $500 to go an entire week without touching? Or $5,000 for an entire month? If you did try to go a month, a week, or even a day without touching, what would be your biggest challenge? Why?

THINK ABOUT IT

3. In a very real sense, our bodies are designed for physical touch. What purpose do the tiny tactile receptors located throughout the body serve? How do they work with the brain? What is the result of their being arranged in clusters, instead of being spread evenly throughout the body?

4. What does Dr. Chapman mean when he says, **"Physical touch can make or break a relationship"**? Give an example of each—preferably from your own experience, if you feel comfortable doing so.

5. Dr. Chapman warns, **"Don't insist on touching [your spouse] in your way and in your time."** You may think a heartfelt high five communicates love; they may find it too casual. You may think the time is right for sexual foreplay; they may consider it self-serving on your part. Give some other examples of physical touch that may not have the desired effect.

6. According to Dr. Chapman, when it comes to learning the love language of physical touch, **"your best instructor is your spouse."** You can send a powerful message of love to your husband or wife by being eager to learn which types of touch communicate love to him or her and which types don't. The way you choose to learn is up to you. On the one hand, their touch preferences may seem like an odd thing to take notes on. On the other hand, it may seem like an odd thing *not* to take notes on. After all, what could be more important in your relationship? With that in mind, what can you do to help facilitate the learning process?

7. What is the difference between explicit love touches and implicit love touches? What would be an ideal scenario for an explicit touch? What would be an ideal scenario for an implicit touch?

8. The story of Joe and Maria reminds us of the importance of communication, especially when it comes to love languages. After their "honeymoon" period, how did the two of them begin to drift apart? What parallels, if any, do you see in your own relationship? Was there a time when you and your spouse seemed to be drifting apart? If so, what happened? What was at the heart of the problem?

9. Dr. Chapman writes this about Joe and Maria: **"Once Joe and Maria discovered they were not meeting each other's need for love, they began to turn things around."** Maria said, "It was like I had a new husband." What potential can you unlock in your relationship by learning your spouse's love language? What would be the best-case scenario for you?

TAKE IT HOME

"In marriage, the touch of love may take many forms. Since touch receptors are located throughout the body, lovingly touching your spouse almost anywhere can be an expression of love." With these words of Dr. Chapman in mind, consider the universe of possibilities available to you as you learn to speak the love language of physical touch.

Using arrows to point to the corresponding body parts, write down as many ideas as you can think of for showing love to your husband or wife through physical touch. Consider everything from brushing your spouse's hair to giving him or her a foot massage.

MAXIMIZING YOUR TOUCH POTENTIAL

Below you'll find charts representing a normal weekday, a normal Saturday, and a normal Sunday in your household. Each chart is divided into six four-hour increments. For each one, estimate the number of physical touches you give your husband or wife during that time period. Give a few examples of the types of touches you might give during that time. For example, from 6:00 a.m. to 10:00 a.m. on a weekday, you might give a good morning kiss when you wake up and a goodbye kiss when you leave for work. From 10:00 a.m. to 2:00 p.m. on a Saturday, you might sit with your arm around your spouse while you watch your child's soccer game. Or you might playfully wrestle for the hose while you wash the car together. Try to be as accurate as possible in your estimates.

After you've thought about the way things are now, think about the way things could be if you prioritized physical touch with your husband or wife. How many more touches could you squeeze into your weekday evening hours? Or your Saturday afternoons? Or your Sunday mornings? What additional types of touches can you add to your repertoire?

NORMAL WEEKDAY

	NUMBER OF TOUCHES ON A NORMAL DAY	TYPES OF TOUCHES ON A NORMAL DAY	POTENTIAL NUMBER OF TOUCHES	ADDITIONAL TYPES OF TOUCHES TO TRY
6:00 a.m. to 10:00 a.m.				
10:00 a.m. to 2:00 p.m.				
2:00 p.m. to 6:00 p.m.				
6:00 p.m. to 10:00 p.m.				
10:00 p.m. to 2:00 a.m.				
2:00 a.m. to 6:00 a.m.				

SATURDAY

	NUMBER OF TOUCHES ON A NORMAL DAY	TYPES OF TOUCHES ON A NORMAL DAY	POTENTIAL NUMBER OF TOUCHES	ADDITIONAL TYPES OF TOUCHES TO TRY
6:00 a.m. to 10:00 a.m.				
10:00 a.m. to 2:00 p.m.				
2:00 p.m. to 6:00 p.m.				
6:00 p.m. to 10:00 p.m.				
10:00 p.m. to 2:00 a.m.				
2:00 a.m. to 6:00 a.m.				

SUNDAY

	NUMBER OF TOUCHES ON A NORMAL DAY	TYPES OF TOUCHES ON A NORMAL DAY	POTENTIAL NUMBER OF TOUCHES	ADDITIONAL TYPES OF TOUCHES TO TRY
6:00 a.m. to 10:00 a.m.				
10:00 a.m. to 2:00 p.m.				
2:00 p.m. to 6:00 p.m.				
6:00 p.m. to 10:00 p.m.				
10:00 p.m. to 2:00 a.m.				
2:00 a.m. to 6:00 a.m.				

LOVE CHALLENGE

The story of Joe and Maria offers a powerful reminder of the relationship-changing potential of physical touch. With that in mind, what changes will you make to your daily routine this week to express love to your spouse through physical touch?

Use this space for more notes, quotes, or lessons learned from the chapter.

OBJECTIVE

In reading this chapter, you will learn how to examine your personal preferences and interactions with your spouse to discover your primary love language.

DISCOVERING YOUR PRIMARY LOVE LANGUAGE

INSTRUCTIONS: Complete this ninth lesson after reading chapter 9 ("Discovering Your Primary Love Language," pp. 119–128) of *The 5 Love Languages*.

KEY
TERM

Negative use of love languages: love language elements that are used in hurtful, damaging ways—or that are simply absent in a relationship—that underscore the importance of their positive use.

OPENING QUESTIONS

1. An ancient Greek maxim advises, "Know thyself." In what areas have you been successful in accomplishing that goal? For example, do you have a sense of how much inner strength you truly possess? Or how much compassion? If so, what circumstances helped you understand yourself better?

2. When was the last time you discovered something new about yourself—or the last time someone pointed out something surprising about you that you'd never realized before?

THINK ABOUT IT

3. Based on what you've learned about words of affirmation, how likely is it that it's your primary love language? What happens—inside you and in your relationship—when you receive words of affirmation? What happens when you go for long periods without receiving words of affirmation?

4. Based on what you've learned about quality time, how likely is it that it's your primary love language? What happens—inside you and in your relationship—when you spend quality time with your spouse? What happens when you go for long periods without spending quality time together?

5. Based on what you've learned about receiving gifts, how likely is it that it's your primary love language? What happens—inside you and in your relationship—when you receive meaningful gifts from your spouse? What happens when you go for long periods without receiving meaningful gifts?

6. Based on what you've learned about acts of service, how likely is it that it's your primary love language? What happens—inside you and in your relationship—when your spouse performs acts of service for you? What happens when he or she neglects to perform acts of service for you?

7. Based on what you've learned about physical touch, how likely is it that it's your primary love language? What happens—inside you and in your relationship—when your spouse looks for ways to give you physical touch? What happens when you go for long periods without receiving physical touch?

8. Why is it understandable for men to assume that physical touch is their primary love language when, in fact, it may not be? How can you and your spouse tell the difference between the biological need for sex and the emotional need of a love language?

9. What does Dr. Chapman say are the three most important questions to answer if you're not sure what your primary love language is? Having considered all three questions, what conclusions have you reached about your primary love language?

TAKE IT HOME

If you're not sure what your primary love language is, answering the following questions may shed some light. Or, for a fuller experience, visit www.5LoveLanguages.com/quizzes to learn your love language.

If you really want to show love to your husband or wife, which of the following would you be most likely to do?

a. Say something from the bottom of your heart or write your feelings in a card.
b. Clear your schedule to spend time alone with him or her.
c. Spend hours shopping online or in stores for a gift that he or she will love.
d. Do household chores that you know will make his or her life easier.
e. Give him or her a back rub.

Which of the following would mean the most to you?

a. You overhear your spouse telling someone how amazingly creative you are.
b. They plan a picnic lunch for the two of you.
c. They surprise you with the perfect gift.
d. They wash your car for you.
e. They initiate a night of lovemaking.

Which of the following would be most emotionally painful to you?

a. Your spouse says something that they know will hurt you.
b. They say they are too busy to spend time with you.
c. They put zero effort into getting a gift for your birthday.
d. They refuse to help you with household responsibilities.
e. They avoid physical contact with you.

What most likely was/is your mother's primary love language?

a. Words of affirmation
b. Quality time
c. Receiving gifts
d. Acts of service
e. Physical touch

What do you base your answer on?

What most likely was/is your father's primary love language?

    a. Words of affirmation
    b. Quality time
    c. Receiving gifts
    d. Acts of service
    e. Physical touch

What do you base your answer on?

If you circled one letter more often than the others, it's likely that the corresponding love language is your primary love language.

LOVE CHALLENGE

Discovering your primary love language is important; helping your husband or wife understand it is essential. How will you initiate a conversation about your love language with your spouse this week? How will you respond if they ask, "What does this mean for me?"

Use this space for more notes, quotes, or lessons learned from the chapter.

OBJECTIVE

In reading this chapter, you will learn how to choose to love
your spouse rather than relying on feelings of love to motivate you.

LOVE IS A CHOICE

INSTRUCTIONS: Complete this tenth lesson after reading chapter 10 ("Love Is a Choice," pp. 131–139) of *The 5 Love Languages*.

KEY TERM

Emotional contentment: ideal marital state in which both spouses' deepest emotional needs are being met, they feel secure in each other's love, and they give their creative energies to wholesome projects outside the marriage while they continue to keep their relationship growing and exciting.

OPENING QUESTIONS

1. How many choices do you suppose you make in an average day? Give some examples of daily choices that you make almost instantaneously and others that require thought and planning.

2. Where do you turn when you have an extremely difficult choice to make? Whose input matters to you? What core principles, beliefs, and priorities guide your decision-making?

THINK ABOUT IT

3. What were the circumstances that brought Brent and Becky to Dr. Chapman's office? Why did Brent's actions come as such a terrible surprise to Becky? In her explanation to Dr. Chapman, what seems to be Becky's only clue that something wasn't quite right in their relationship?

4. What happened during Brent and Becky's twelve years of marriage that led them to that point? Do you see any parallels to your own relationship? If so, what insight or advice would you have offered Becky? If not, why did your relationship take a different turn?

5. Brent's blunt admission of his feelings toward his wife—"I just don't love her anymore"—may seem cruel. But Dr. Chapman says, **"I sympathized with Brent, for I have been there."** What does he mean by "there"?

6. According to Dr. Chapman, the in-love experience **"seems to serve for humankind the same function as the mating call of the Canada goose."** It's something that happens naturally in the normal context of romantic relationships. Why is it a mistake to believe that the in-love experience will last forever?

7. What choice do couples face when they come down from the natural high of the in-love experience?

8. What does Dr. Chapman identify as his wife's primary love language? What is one of his key strategies for speaking that love language? Why is that particular strategy especially challenging for him? Why does that make his strategy even more impactful for his wife?

9. On a scale of one to ten, with ten being the highest, how well-equipped are you to communicate in your spouse's primary love language? Explain. On a scale of one to ten, with ten being the highest, how motivated are you to learn their primary love language? Explain.

TAKE IT HOME

For each love language, think of a reason a spouse might choose not to learn it. For example, for physical touch, they might say, "I'm not a toucher. I never saw my mother and father hug each other. They never hugged me. I'm just not comfortable with it."

Then think of a better reason a spouse might choose to learn the love language. For example, they might say, "If an act of service brings my wife the kind of pleasure I get from the physical touch of sexual intercourse, then I'm happy to do laundry."

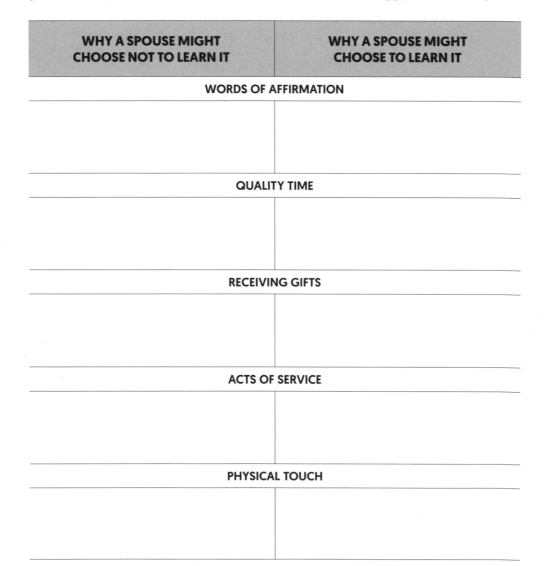

WHY A SPOUSE MIGHT CHOOSE NOT TO LEARN IT	WHY A SPOUSE MIGHT CHOOSE TO LEARN IT
WORDS OF AFFIRMATION	
QUALITY TIME	
RECEIVING GIFTS	
ACTS OF SERVICE	
PHYSICAL TOUCH	

TIMELINE

"Love doesn't erase the past, but it makes the future different." To fully appreciate the potential in that sentence, you need to consider your specific past, present, and future—the timeline of your relationship with your spouse.

On the timeline below, mark some of the major past events, highlights, or periods of your relationship. For example, some couples experience the "Seven-Year Itch." Maybe you experienced the "Six-Month Honeymoon" or the "One-Year Break" or the "Two-Year Constant Argument" or the "Three-Year Boredom" or the "Eight-Year Staying Together for the Kids."

After you've marked the past section, turn your attention to the future. Think of milestones you anticipate reaching with your husband or wife once both of your love tanks are full. They might include anything from recapturing the giddiness of your early days of dating to encouraging one another to reach specific personal goals to celebrating your golden anniversary surrounded by your family and friends.

PAST   **You are here.**   **FUTURE**

LOVE CHALLENGE

Dr. Chapman concludes the chapter with these words: **"Love is a choice. And either partner can start the process today."** What will you do this week to communicate to your spouse that you know his or her primary love language and that you choose to speak it?

Use this space for more notes, quotes, or lessons learned from the chapter.

OBJECTIVE

In reading this chapter, you will learn how love allows couples to resolve conflict, live together in harmony, and bring out the best in each other.

LOVE MAKES THE DIFFERENCE

INSTRUCTIONS: Complete this eleventh lesson after reading chapter 11 ("Love Makes the Difference," pp. 141–147) of *The 5 Love Languages*.

KEY TERM

Basic needs: the core necessities— including love, security, self-worth, and significance—that must be present if we are to have emotional well-being.

OPENING QUESTIONS

1. What songs "tell your love story"—that is, what songs describe how you feel about your spouse or your relationship or your attitude toward love?

2. Describe the emotional and physical differences you notice in yourself when you're in a loving relationship versus after you've broken up with a partner or spent a lot of time single. How do you explain those differences?

THINK ABOUT IT

3. Everyone has a basic need for security. What does that need look like in your life? What events or circumstances in your past have made you feel secure or less than secure? How is your daily life different when you have a sense of security from when you don't have that sense?

4. Everyone has a basic need for self-worth. What does that need look like in your life? What events or circumstances in your past have made you feel valuable or worthless? How is your daily life different when you have a sense of being valuable from when you don't have that sense?

5. Everyone has a basic need for significance. What does that need look like in your life? What events or circumstances in your past have made you feel that you're a success or that you have great potential? What events or circumstances in your past have made you feel like a failure or that you have little potential? How is your daily life different when you feel like a potential success from when you feel like a failure?

6. How does your spouse affect your sense of security, either in a positive way or a negative way? How do they affect your self-worth? How do they affect your sense of significance?

7. What could your spouse do to make you feel more secure? What could they do to make you feel more valued or worthwhile? What could they do to make you feel more significant or important?

8. How would your spouse say you affect their sense of security? How would they say you affect their self-worth? How would they say you affect their sense of significance or importance?

9. It's an awesome realization to know that we can help meet our spouse's most basic human needs and impact him or her at the very core of his or her being. It's also an awesome responsibility—one we can't take lightly. What changes can you make to your daily routine to help your husband or wife feel more secure? What changes can you make to help them feel more valued or worthwhile? What changes can you make to help them feel more significant or important?

TAKE IT HOME

In Dr. Chapman's story about John and Susan, Susan didn't feel any love coming from John. This frustrated John, who saw himself as showing all kinds of loving actions toward Susan. Figuratively speaking, he seemed to be firing arrow after arrow at the target of Susan's love language. He prepared dinner. He vacuumed. He did the yard work. He folded clothes. The problem was, John was aiming at the wrong target. He assumed Susan's love language was acts of service because that was his love language. It's a common mistake. Chances are, you've made a similar one. We all have.

On the target below, write the love language that you mistakenly assumed was your spouse's primary language. Draw and label arrows to indicate the different ways you tried to speak that love language and show love to them. For example, let's say you assumed their love language was physical touch. You might have tried back rubs, holding hands while you walk together, and hugs all to no avail.

THE RIGHT TARGET

When John learned that Susan's actual primary love language was quality time—with the specific dialect of quality conversation—he was able to be more accurate with his "arrows." Armed with similar knowledge, you can be more accurate as well. On the target below, write your spouse's actual primary love language. Draw and label arrows to indicate ways you can show love to him or her in a way that resonates powerfully.

LOVE CHALLENGE

The story of John and Susan illustrates the dangers of assuming that your spouse knows what you need. What will you say to your husband or wife this week to help them understand what you need to feel more secure, more worthwhile, or more significant?

Use this space for more notes, quotes, or lessons learned from the chapter.

OBJECTIVE

In reading this chapter, you will learn how to love an enemy—specifically,
a spouse who seems determined to be as unlovable as possible.

LOVING THE UNLOVELY

LESSON

12

INSTRUCTIONS: Complete this twelfth lesson after reading chapter 12 ("Loving the Unlovely," pp. 149–163) of *The 5 Love Languages*.

KEY TERM

The unlovely: a husband or wife who no longer shows love to his or her spouse due to an empty love tank and who makes it difficult for his or her spouse to continue the relationship.

OPENING QUESTIONS

1. What do you consider your greatest accomplishment? What kind of challenges, hard work, and sacrifice were part of that accomplishment?

2. How does having that accomplishment under your belt affect your self-confidence, especially when it comes to facing other challenges?

THINK ABOUT IT

3. When two people get married in the throes of the in-love experience, they don't think of marriage as a challenge. They assume the honeymoon will last forever. How can that naive approach to marriage eventually lead to the kind of situation Glenn and Ann faced in their relationship?

4. Dr. Chapman empathized with Glenn and Ann's situation. His candid confession about him and his wife experiencing feelings of hatred in the early days of their own marriage illustrates just how common it is for the challenges of marriage to get the better of our emotions. What does he say led to those feelings of hatred? What made the difference for him and his wife in overcoming those feelings?

5. Dr. Chapman acknowledged the challenge of following Jesus' command to "love your enemies, do good to those who hate you, bless those who curse you, pray for those who mistreat you. . . . Do to others as you would have them do to you" (Luke 6:27–28, 31). How is that challenge magnified when the "enemy" is your own spouse?

6. What was the six-month experiment that Dr. Chapman recommended
    to Ann? Which part of the plan do you think was most difficult for her?
    Explain. What does Ann's willingness to go through with the experiment say
    about her?

7. How do you think your husband or wife would respond if you asked for
    suggestions for how you could do a better job of meeting their emotional
    needs, as Ann did for Glenn? How do you imagine you would react to
    hearing their suggestions?

8. On a scale of one to ten, with one being "Completely Unmotivated" and ten
    being "Couldn't Be More Eager," how motivated would you be to take your
    spouse's suggestions to heart and do the things he or she requested? How do
    you explain your motivation—or lack thereof?

9. If someone asked you, "Is it possible to love someone you hate?" what
    would your reply be? What reasons would you give for your answer? What
    examples would you give to support your opinion?

TAKE IT HOME

The question Ann asked Dr. Chapman—"Is it possible to love someone you hate?"—drives home the point that many couples fail to consider when they marry: people change. Obviously, Ann and Glenn didn't hate each other on their wedding day; otherwise, they wouldn't have committed themselves to each other for the rest of their lives.

But something happened after the "I dos." Ann and Glenn changed. Maybe they reverted back to the people they were before their courtship. Maybe they brought out aspects of each other that surprised them both. While some changes were probably gradual, others may have been frighteningly quick.

Can you empathize with them? On one side of the illustration below, list some changes you've noticed in yourself since you got married. Be honest, even if some of the changes aren't necessarily flattering. On the other side, list some changes you've noticed in your spouse.

How have those changes affected your closeness with your husband or wife? Draw stick figures of you and your spouse to show how close the two of you were when you got married. Then draw two more stick figures to show how close the two of you are now.

THE TIES THAT BIND

If you see parallels between Glenn and Ann's relationship and your own, you might want to assess your situation—specifically, what's holding your relationship together. Identifying your "ties that bind" can help you lay the groundwork for saving your relationship.

Using the biblical image of a cord of three strands as a guideline, draw and label the cords that wind together to give your relationship strength. For example, one cord might be the vow you made on your wedding day—the one that says, "For better or worse." Other cords might include your children, your spiritual beliefs, your shared history with your spouse, and your fear of starting over. Use the thickness of each cord to indicate how big of a factor it is in your staying together—the thicker the cord, the bigger the role it plays in holding your relationship intact.

LOVE CHALLENGE

Will you fight to save your relationship? Will you do the difficult, thankless work necessary to fill the love tank of an unmotivated spouse? If so, how will you announce your intentions to them this week? What kind of response do you expect? What will be your reaction?

Use this space for more notes, quotes, or lessons learned from the chapter.

THE 5 LOVE LANGUAGES
LEADER'S GUIDE

Congratulations! You're on the cusp of an exciting adventure. You're about to lead a small group through twelve studies that will enrich relationships and change lives. And you'll have a front-row seat to it all.

You'll find that every small group presents its own unique challenges and opportunities. But there are some tips that can help you get the most out of any small-group study, whether you're a seasoned veteran or a first-time leader.

1. Communicate.

From the outset, you'll want to give members a sense of how your group dynamic will work. To maximize your time together, group members will need to read each lesson's assigned chapter of *The 5 Love Languages* and then complete the "Opening Questions" (questions 1–2) and "Think About It" section (questions 3–9) *before* the meeting. The "Take It Home" and "Love Challenge" activities should be completed after the meeting.

2. Keep a good pace.

Your first meeting will begin with introductions (if necessary). After that, you'll ask group members to share their responses to the first two "Getting Started" questions. These are icebreakers. Their purpose is merely to introduce the session topic. You'll want to give everyone a chance to share, but you don't want to get sidetracked by overly long discussions here.

The "Think About It" section (questions 3–9) is the heart of the study. This is where most of your discussion should occur. You'll need to establish a good pace, making sure that you give each question its due while allowing enough time to tackle all of them. After you've finished your discussion of the questions, briefly go over the "Take It Home" and "Love Challenge" sections so that group members know what their "homework" will be.

Your next meeting will begin with a brief review of that homework. Ask volunteers to share their responses to the "Take It Home" activities and their experiences in implementing the "Love Challenge." After about five minutes of reviewing your group members' application of the previous lesson, begin your new lesson.

3. Prepare.

Read each chapter, answer the study questions, and work through the take-home material, just like your group members will do. Try to anticipate questions or comments your group members will have. If you have time, think of stories from your own relationship or from the relationships of people you know that apply to the lesson. That way, if you have a lull during your study, you can use the stories to spark conversation.

4. Be open and vulnerable.

Not everyone is comfortable with sharing the details of their relationship with other people. Yet openness and vulnerability are essential in a group setting. That's where you come in. If you have the courage to be vulnerable, to share less-than-flattering details about your own relationship (with your spouse's permission, of course), you may give others the courage to do the same.

5. Emphasize and celebrate the uniqueness of every relationship.

Some group members may feel intimidated by other people's seemingly successful relationships. Others may find that strategies for learning love languages that work for some people don't work for them—and they may get discouraged. You can head off that discouragement by opening up about your own struggles and successes. Help group members see that, beneath the surface, every relationship has its challenges.

6. Create a safe haven where people feel free—and comfortable—to share.

Ask group members to agree to some guidelines before your first meeting. For example, what is said in the group setting stays in the group setting. And every person's voice deserves to be heard. If you find that some group members are quick to give unsolicited advice or criticism when other people share, remind the group that every relationship is unique. What works for one may not work for another. If the problem persists, talk with your advice givers and critics one-on-one. Help them see how their well-intended comments may be having the unintended effect of discouraging others from talking.

7. Follow up.

The questions and activities in this book encourage group members to read through *The 5 Love Languages*, initiate difficult conversations with their spouses, and make significant changes to their relationship routines. You can be the cheerleader your group members need by celebrating their successes and congratulating them for their courage and commitment. Also, by checking in each week with your group members, you create accountability and give them motivation to apply *The 5 Love Languages* principles to their relationships.

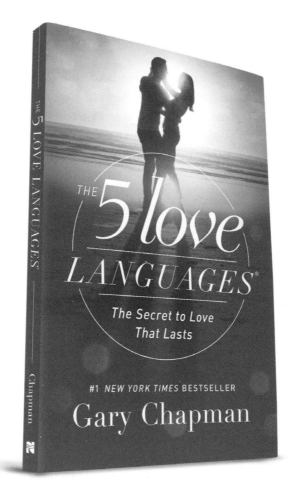

Simple ways to
strengthen relationships.

- TAKE THE LOVE LANGUAGE® QUIZ

- DOWNLOAD FREE RESOURCES AND STUDY GUIDES

- BROWSE THE LOVE LANGUAGE® GIFT GUIDE

- SUBSCRIBE TO PODCASTS

- SHOP THE STORE

- SIGN UP FOR THE NEWSLETTER

Visit www.5lovelanguages.com

FUN, CREATIVE, AND SPIRITUALLY ENGAGING—
THESE ARE NO ORDINARY DATES!

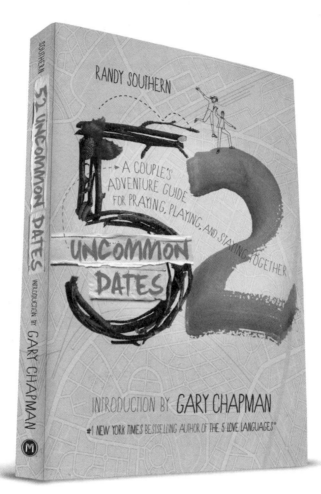

The 5 Love Languages® Mobile App

Your personal assistant for relationships.

- Free and easy set up that only takes a couple of minutes.

- Take the Love Language® Quiz to learn what makes you feel loved.

- Link your app to your partner's to unlock extra features.

- Set goals to help you speak your partner's Love Language® consistently.

- Nudge your partner with helpful messages and requests.

- Track your progress to build healthy habits in your relationship.

Tap a language to learn more about it

37%	Receiving Gifts
29%	Acts of Service
16%	Words of Affirmation
10%	Quality Time
8%	Physical Touch

Continue

Get it on
Google Play

Download on the
App Store

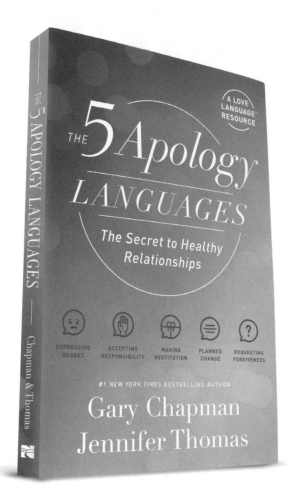